Savvy

POSITIVE REACTION!

A CRASH COURSE IN *Science*

BY SARA L. LATTA

Consultant:
Lynne E. Houtz, MS, PhD
Professor, Associate Chair of Education
Creighton University
Omaha, Nebraska

CAPSTONE PRESS
a capstone imprint

T0081029

Savvy Books are published by Capstone Press,
1710 Roe Crest Drive, North Mankato, Minnesota 56003
www.capstonepub.com

Library of Congress Cataloging-in-Publication Data
Latta, Sara L., author.
  Positive reaction! : a crash course in science / by Sara Latta.
    pages cm. — (Crash course)
  "Savvy Books."
  Summary: "Simplifies junior high science in engaging and conversational language and
offers examples and activities to show readers how the topics tie in to real life"— Provided by
publisher.
Includes and index.
ISBN 978-1-4914-0772-1 (library binding)
ISBN 978-1-4914-0780-6 (paperback)
ISBN 978-1-4914-0776-9 (eBook pdf)
1. Science—Study and teaching (Middle school)—Juvenile literature. 2. Science—Juvenile
literature. I. Title.
  Q163.L315 2015
  507.1′2—dc23
                              2014012078

Editorial Credits
Abby Colich, editor; Lori Bye, designer; Gina Kammer, media researcher;
Kathy McColley, production specialist

Photo Credits
Capstone Press: Bernice Lum, 12; iStockphotos: A-Digit, 16; Shutterstock: Aaron Amat,
9 (bottom), agsandrew, 4, 18, Alex Mit, 20 (left), AlexRoz, 21 (top), Ammit Jack, 51 (left),
andersphoto, 19 (bottom right), Antonio Guillem, 19 (bottom left), Barnaby Chambers, 37,
bikeriderlondon, 21 (bottom), Bildagentur Zoonar GmbH, 31, BlueRingMedia, 23, Carlos
Caetano, 14, cobalt88, 27 (top), Computer Earth, 46, Dean Drobot, 17, Designua, 41, djem
(abstract molecular structure), 53, 58, DnD-Production.com, 34 (right), FomaA, 24 (right),
Fotyma, 9 (middle), Francesco83, 27 (bottom), FTXbg, 33, Getideaka, 54 (top), gualtiero boffi,
22 (bottom), ifong, 51 (right), irin-k, 30 (right), Jakkrit Orrasri, 30 (left), jmcdermottillo (pop
art style faces), cover and throughout, Johan Swanepoel, 38, jopelka, 26 (top), back cover,
Katrina Leigh, 29, Kodda, 48, kosmos111, 39, Kudryashka, (hand-drawn colorful wave pattern),
throughout, Lipowski Milan, 25 (top), magicoven, 13 (top), MANDY GODBEHEAR, 58 (bottom),
Mara008, 8, marre, 13 (bottom), MichaelTaylor, 35 (left), ndoeljindoel, 57 (left), nico99, 34 (left),
Olga Danylenko, 43, Panu Ruangjan, 22 (top), PathDoc, 56 (left), Pete Saloutos, 10, back cover,
PhotoSGH, 50, Pushish Donhongsa, 19 (top), racorn, 57 (right), Rainbow-Pic, 21 (middle),
Roxana Bashyrova, 26 (middle), Sam Chadwick, 49, schankz, 24 (left), 45, Scisetti Alfio, 9 (top),
SCOTTCHAN, 42, Sergio33, 25 (bottom), snapgalleria, 7, 32, 44, Stanislav Tiplyashin, 28, Steshkin
Yevgeniy, 20 (right), Steve Cukrov, 54 (bottom), stockyimages, 52, Syda Productions, 56 (right),
TaraPatta, 53 (top), terekhov igor, 15, udaix, 40, Vikpit, 26 (bottom), vilax, 35 (right), violetblue, 6,
vipman, 55, Vlad61, 47
Design elements: Shutterstock

Printed in the United States of America in Stevens Point, Wisconsin.
032014   008092WZF14

Table of Contents

SAVVY ABOUT SCIENCE

Think science is a collection of dusty, dry facts? Think again. It's actually a way of investigating some of the most pressing questions about our selves, our world, and our universe.

Do you want to find out why your hair gets frizzy when it rains? Or how to pull off an awesome spin at the skating rink? You'll find the answers in science. Science is a never-ending quest to understand the natural world.

You're about to take a crash course in the different areas of science you'll study in school. Wonder how the world works? Try learning some chemistry and physics. What makes us and other living things tick? Think life sciences. Want to explore the farthest reaches of outer space? Then earth and space sciences are your new best friends. Love making cool stuff? Then put engineering on the top of your list. You may not realize it, but science is a part of your everyday life. And here's how.

HOW TO USE THIS BOOK

This book is designed so you can read the chapters in any order you like. If you have a biology, chemistry, or physics assignment, you can find that section quickly and get the information you need presented in a fun, easy-to-understand way. Each chapter has fun activities and questions to test your knowledge. You'll find answers on pages 60–61.

CHAPTER 1

It's All About Matter: The Physical Sciences

One of your friends is having a few people over for her birthday. You walk in and follow your nose to the food. You find the pizza. Mmm! You might not realize it, but that pizza and everything you can see, touch, smell, taste, or feel is made of matter. Matter is anything that has mass and takes up space. Think of our world like the party at your friend's house. The basic building blocks of matter, called atoms, and the forces that hold them together are like people at a party. They constantly bump into one another and move from one social group to another.

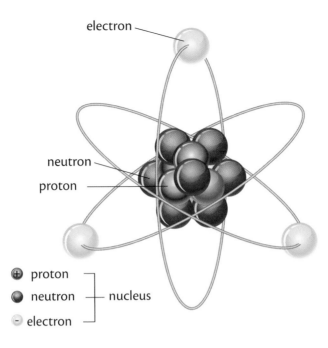

electron

neutron

proton

proton

neutron — nucleus

electron

Atoms are the smallest possible pieces of matter. At the center of each atom is the nucleus. Inside the nucleus of most atoms are two types of particles—protons and neutrons. Protons have a positive electrical charge. Neutrons have no charge. You wouldn't go to a party without any clothes, right? The nucleus is normally surrounded by negatively charged particles called electrons that whirl about in all directions. Some party clothes!

QUICK TIP

Protons start with "p" and have a positive charge. Neutrons start with "n" and have no charge, or are neutral.

WHEN ATOMS GET TOGETHER

At any party there are many different personalities. Different substances, like people, each have their own personalities too. Some, like helium, like to keep to themselves. You won't find helium atoms interacting with other atoms. It has all of the electrons it can handle. And it's not sharing any either.

Others atoms, such as oxygen, are more social. They can bond with other atoms by sharing electrons. The oxygen that we breathe is actually a pair of oxygen atoms bonded to each other, abbreviated O_2. Think of them as identical twins who really enjoy each other's company. Together they form an oxygen molecule.

Oxygen atoms are friendly with other atoms too. An oxygen molecule can join a carbon atom to form carbon dioxide, or CO_2. Carbon dioxide is the gas we breathe out of our lungs.

Experiment

You'll need:
- one balloon
- an empty 16 ounce (480 milliliter) soda bottle
- white vinegar
- baking soda

Steps:

Pour ¼ cup (60 mL) of vinegar into the soda bottle.

Have a friend hold the mouth of a balloon open while you pour a teaspoon of baking soda into the balloon.

Stretch the mouth of the balloon over the bottle, keeping the main part of the balloon drooping off to the side. Ready for some fun? Hold tight to the connection between the balloon and the bottle as you dump the baking soda into the bottle, and watch the balloon inflate!

What just happened? What do you think would happen if you added more or less baking soda to the vinegar?

Other atoms form bonds by transferring electrons to another atom. The sodium atom (Na) has an electron in its outer shell that it desperately wants to get rid of. Sodium, meet chlorine, who desperately wants to grab onto that extra electron. This friendship results in sodium chloride, or NaCl, known as table salt.

9

"A FORCE TO BE RECKONED WITH"

Have you ever heard this phrase about someone who is really powerful and important? You're "a force to be reckoned with" too. So is everything in the universe.

Some forces hold things together. Others push them apart. Some can do both. If you kick a soccer ball down the field, you are applying a force to it. Score!

Kicking a soccer ball is an example of a contact force. You applied direct force to the object, and it moved. Friction is another contact force. It comes from the interaction of two bumpy surfaces. (The bumps can be very slight.) If you've ever slipped and fallen on an icy sidewalk, you know that frozen water offers little friction. The greater the mass of an object, the more force it takes to move it. That's why we kick around soccer balls and not rocks!

The force of gravity pulls you down toward the center of Earth. Gravity holds Earth and the other planets in orbit around the sun.

Things with positive or negative charges can exert electrical forces. Things with like charges repel each other. Opposite charges attract. Magnetic forces are actually created by spinning electrons. These two forces are closely related, so we often call them electromagnetic forces.

QUICK TIP
Forces push or pull. Some require contact. Others don't.

IT'S THE LAW!

You make it home at 10:59 p.m., one minute before your weekend curfew. It's the rule, after all. There are rules and laws in science too.

Sir Isaac Newton, born in 1643, was a supersmart scientist. You may have heard that he got his idea about gravity when an apple fell on his head. That story may not be true, but he did come up with some pretty amazing ideas about force and motion. Today we call them Newton's Three Laws of Motion.

Newton's First Law of Motion has two parts. The first part states that an object at rest stays at rest, unless acted upon by an unbalanced force. Think of a couch potato. The second part says that an object in motion continues in motion with the same speed and in the same direction unless acted upon by an unbalanced force.

Newton's Second Law of Motion states that when you apply a force to anything with mass, like when you kick a soccer ball, you cause acceleration. The acceleration depends on the amount of force applied. The more mass an object has, the more force is required to move it. The harder you kick, the faster the ball moves.

Newton's Third Law of Motion says that for every action, there is an equal and opposite reaction. In other words, if you push an object, it pushes back in the opposite direction equally hard.

Experiment

To see Newton's third law in action, try this fun demonstration.

You'll need:
- ruler with a center groove
- 7 marbles of the same size
- tape

Steps:

Tape the ruler to a table or countertop with a level surface.

Place five marbles along the center groove. Make sure that they touch each other.

Roll a sixth marble down the groove into the other marbles. Now try rolling two marbles at a time into the row.

What's happening? When your moving marble runs into the row of marbles, it transfers its force to the row of marbles. When you roll two marbles into the row, you're applying twice as much force to the row.

It's Monday morning. Your alarm goes off at 7:00 a.m. But you just don't have the energy to bounce out of bed. You hear about energy all the time. Energy is something that is used to do work—to cause some sort of change. Like matter, energy can't be created or destroyed. It can only be stored or transferred.

Have you ever ridden a roller coaster? At the very top of the hill, the car you're riding in has a lot of stored energy. That's called potential energy.

As you begin your plunge downward, your car's potential energy is converted into kinetic energy. Anything that moves—from planets to atoms—has kinetic energy.

Chemical energy is stored in the bonds of atoms and molecules. Think of toasting marshmallows over a bonfire. The energy from the fire breaks the bonds of the marshmallow's sugar molecules, making it all toasty brown. Yum! Your body uses the chemical energy stored in the sugar to do things like power your muscles and keep your body warm.

Remember those negatively charged particles called electrons? Moving electrons have a kind of kinetic energy called electrical energy. Even before people knew about electricity, they were surrounded by electrical energy. Lightning is one example of electrical energy. So is the static electricity that makes your socks cling to your skirt.

By now you may suspect that forces and energy are closely related. You're right! Energy is really the ability to apply force over a certain distance. A bowling ball rolling down the lane has kinetic energy. When it hits the pins, it uses that energy to exert a force to knock them over.

Experiment

See the transfer of energy in action with the experiment.

You'll need:
- a large ball such as a basketball or soccer ball
- a smaller, lighter ball such as a tennis ball or table tennis ball

Steps:

Make sure you're outside with plenty of room. Hold one hand under the larger ball, and the other hand on top of the smaller ball. The smaller ball should be sitting directly on top of the larger ball. Let go of both balls at the same time.

When the larger ball hits the ground, you should see that the smaller ball bounces off the larger one and flies high into the air. What's happening here?

MAKING WAVES

You resisted the urge to hit that snooze button and made it school on time. Before your first class, you spot some friends. They wave, and you wave back. Whether you know it or not, you're surrounded by waves and not just the "hey, good to see you" kind.

Some waves you can see, such as ocean waves. Other kinds you can't see, such as sound waves and light waves. Waves are a way of transferring energy from one place to another—without transferring matter.

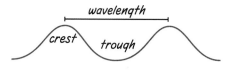

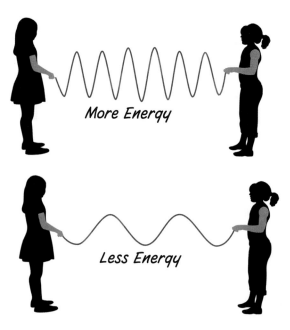

Ever used a jump rope? Then you've probably used the rope to create a wave. Your friend holds one end while you jiggle the other end up and down.

The wavelength is the distance between two neighboring crests, or highest points, of the wave. If you jiggle your jump rope faster, you'll make shorter wavelengths. It takes more energy to make those waves, right? If you jiggle your jump rope more slowly, the wavelength is longer—and it has less energy. The more waves that pass a given point in a second, the higher the frequency of the wavelength. The height of the wave, from the trough to the crest is called the amplitude.

SOUND WAVES

Sound waves need to move through some sort of physical stuff in order to transfer energy. Ocean waves need water, stadium waves need people, and sound waves need air. Sound waves are produced when something vibrates. A flute player blowing air into her instrument sets up a vibration, or sound wave. Those vibrations nudge the air molecules next to the flute. They travel in waves, each molecule bumping into the next. When those sound waves reach our eardrums, they start to vibrate too.

Light Waves and Electromagnetic Energy

The light that we can see is one example of electromagnetic energy, or electromagnetic radiation. Electromagnetic waves are formed by the vibrations of electric and magnetic fields. They're related, remember? Unlike sound waves, electromagnetic waves don't need matter to transfer their energy.

QUICK TIP

Radiation is simply energy that travels and spreads out as it goes.

Electromagnetic waves range from super-short—a few fraction of a millimeter—to longer than a mile. The shorter the wavelength the more energy it carries—just like sound waves. The greater the amplitude of the wavelength, the more intense the light. We call this range of wavelengths the electromagnetic spectrum. All electromagnetic radiation is light, but our eyes can only tune the wavelengths of a small band of the spectrum.

Radiation Is Everywhere

Your dentist uses X-rays to look at your teeth. You use microwaves to make popcorn or heat a bowl of soup. You use radio waves when you watch TV or use your cell phone. When you do these things, you are using electromagnetic energy.

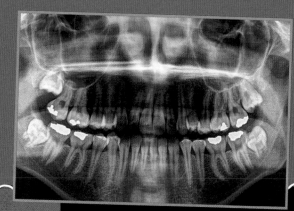

Experiment

See the transfer of energy in action with the experiment.

You'll need:
- some clean laundry
- a clothes drier
- a portable radio with an AM dial

Steps:

With your parents' permission, put some clean laundry, including socks, into the clothes dryer. Don't use any antistatic products, and run the drier as usual. Place a portable radio on top of the dryer and tune it in to an AM station. Once your clothes are dry, pull them out of the dryer. You'll notice that some of them, especially the socks, are clinging together. As you pull them apart, you'll hear a faint crackling sound—and also some static on the radio. What is causing this?

TEST YOUR SCIENCE SAVVY

1. Which of Newton's Laws explains why you should always wear your seat belt?

2. A rainbow is an example of what kind of wave?

3. A softball player slides into home plate. She slows down as a result of what kind of force?

CHAPTER 2

WE'RE ALL IN THIS TOGETHER: LIFE SCIENCES

You probably have a lot of things in common with your friends. Maybe you like the same kind of music, are crazy about soccer, or laugh at the same jokes. You also have a lot in common with elephants, mushrooms, roses, bees, and even bacteria. They're living things, just like you.

Sold on Cells

Living things are made up of one or more cells. Elephants have a lot. So do you. Bacteria and many other organisms do fine with just one cell. Most cells are a tiny fraction of an inch across—much too small to be seen without a microscope.

All cells have a membrane that protects them from the outside world. There are specialized channels that move stuff in and out of the cell. Inside, cells have structures called organelles. These each have a special job that keep the cell alive and working. Mitochondria are the powerhouses of the cell. They generate energy-rich molecules to keep the cell running. Other organelles are like food warehouses and waste management plants.

Plant and animal cells have a nucleus. The nucleus contains DNA (deoxyribonucleic acid). DNA is organized in large structures called chromosomes. DNA stores all of our genetic information. It determines the color of your eyes, whether your hair is curly or straight, and even your ability to roll your tongue. DNA also acts like the manager in a factory. It gives instructions that tell your cells what to do.

Anatomy of an Animal Cell

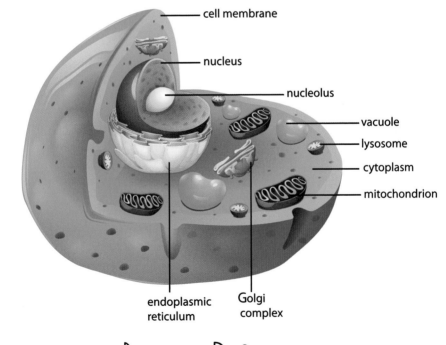

cell membrane

nucleus

nucleolus

vacuole

lysosome

cytoplasm

mitochondrion

endoplasmic reticulum

Golgi complex

Bonus Point

You have specialized skin cells, blood cells, and muscle cells. Can you think of other types of cells in your body?

ENERGY FOR LiFE

Living things need energy to keep things running, to make new parts and repair damaged ones. Animals (that includes you!) get their energy and the building materials they need to survive from eating other animals or plants. Mushrooms and other fungi absorb ready-made food from what's around them, such as a rotting log.

Plants, algae, and many microbes get the building materials they need from air and water. They use the energy from the sun to make their own food. This is called photosynthesis.

Rad Responses

Living things respond to their surroundings. Sunflowers turn their faces to follow the sun. Ants follow the smell of food to your picnic. You shiver when it's cold and sweat when it's hot. Your senses send messages to your brain. You respond in ways that help keep you safe and alive.

QUICK TIP

Lizards and other cold-blooded animals can control their body temperature by basking in the warm sun.

REPRODUCTION

Living things grow and reproduce. Reproduction is not essential for individuals, but it must occur for a species to survive. For some living things, just one parent can have offspring. Many single-celled organisms reproduce this way. So do strawberries and starfish. The offspring have the same genetic material as the parent.

Other living things combine the genetic material of a male and a female parent. Mom's strand of DNA combines with Dad's DNA strand. They wrap around each other, separate, and then recombine. They swap individual genes and groups of genes. Mutations—slight "mistakes" in the genes that may or may not be harmful—can produce even more differences. The result is a new double-stranded DNA molecule that is different from both parents. You inherit specific traits from each parent, but you're also uniquely you.

Experiment

Play the telephone game with a bunch of your friends. Think of a phrase and whisper it into the ear of the person next to you—just once. For example, "Hi everyone. I'm Olga, and I like warm bugs." She must whisper it into the ear of the person next to her. The last person in the group says the phrase aloud. Chances are, the message changed somewhere along the line.

These changes are like mutations. If you play the game with a different group of friends, you'll probably end up with a different phrase. This is an example of how different populations can become genetically diverse.

ADAPTATION

Living things have the ability to adapt to their environments. If you have your heart set on becoming an awesome guitar player, you'll spend hours and hour practicing. Over time, you might get to be a pretty mean guitar player. That's adaptation. But if your fingers are short and stubby, you might not be able to play all of the chords. You can adapt and work with what you have. But you can't change your genetic makeup.

Adaptation Means Change

Entire species also adapt to their environments in a process called natural selection. Living things that are better adapted to their environment are more successful at surviving. They also produce more offspring.

All it takes is a quick look around your classroom to confirm that no two humans are alike. It's the same with plants and animals in the wild. One field mouse may look like another to you. But it's a pretty safe bet that some are better at finding a tasty morsel, while others are better at hiding from a hungry hawk. When resources become scarce, those who are better adapted to their environment tend to survive and pass on their genes. Over millions of years, a species may change, or evolve, into a new species.

Let's Review!

Living things …
• have one or more cells
• need energy
• respond to their surroundings
• grow and reproduce
• adapt to their environments

ECOSYSTEMS: LIVING TOGETHER!

You're working on group project, and everyone is assigned a certain task. You know everyone must work together as a team, or you may not get the assignment finished.

Ecosystems work together like a team too. Some members of an ecosystem team include nonliving things such as soil, water, air, temperature, and sunlight. These are called abiotic factors. The other members are made up of biotic factors. These are things that are alive, or were once alive. A living tree, a decaying stump, the remains of a mouse, a buzzing fly, microbes, and fungi are all examples of biotic factors. All abiotic and biotic factors interact in some way to form an ecosystem. Ecosystems can be small, such as a puddle of water, or huge, such as an entire forest.

Groups of the same species living in the same ecosystem are called populations. Different species living in the same population form a community. They all play important roles in the ecosystem. In ecosystems there is often competition. Individuals have to compete for limited food, space, or light.

QUICK TIP

Here's an easy way to remember the abiotic factors—soil, water, air, temperature, and sunlight: SWATS!

FOOD WEBS

When you bite into your sandwich at lunch, do you think about where your food comes from? The farm to the factory to the store to your plate. It's all one big cycle. Nature has its own food cycle too. Each living thing in an ecosystem is part of a food chain. Several food chains are connected together to form a food web. Organisms in food webs fall into three basic categories.

The first are the producers. Plants are the most familiar producers. Whenever you eat a fruit or a vegetable, you're eating a producer. During photosynthesis producers convert sunlight into energy. Their roots pull nutrients from the soil and use them for energy too.

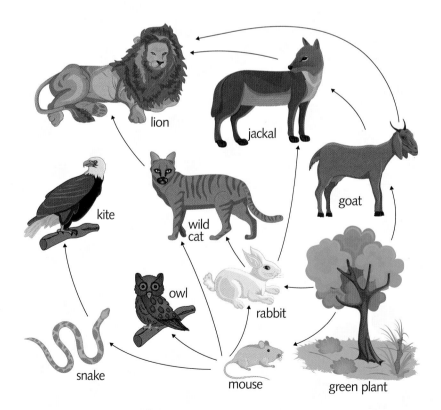

lion

jackal

goat

kite

wild cat

owl

rabbit

snake

mouse

green plant

Next are the consumers, which eat the producers. You're a consumer whenever you eat a producer. Deer, mice, cows are all primary consumers. Primary consumers can also be food for other consumers. The mouse might be a meal for a snake, which in turn might end up in the stomach of an owl. These are called secondary consumers. On it goes to the top of the food chain. Lions and great white sharks are examples of consumers at the top of the food chain. They have no natural enemies (other than humans).

Scavengers, such as vultures, eat dead meat or rotting plant material. Decomposers—fungi and bacteria—break dead plants and animals into even smaller pieces, eventually returning all of those molecules back to the earth. The cycle is complete.

Losing Balance

Ecosystems are healthy when the producers, consumers, and decomposers are all in balance. There can be real problems if that balance is disrupted. For example, invasive species such as the Asian carp imported into the United States have taken over some rivers. They have huge appetites, eating so many plants and other producers that they starve out the other fish. Human development has destroyed the habitat for many top predators. Ecosystems are at risk until humans do more to protect them and restore balance.

TEST YOUR SCIENCE SAVVY

1. The definition of life can be tricky. Can you think of a living thing that does not meet all of the definitions of life? Can you think of some nonliving things that follow at least some of the rules?

2. A Venus flytrap plant gets its energy from the sun and carries out photosynthesis. It also traps and consumes flies and other insects. Is the Venus flytrap a

A. producer
B. consumer
C. both A and B

3. What do plants need to carry out photosynthesis?

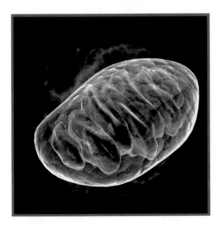

4. Which organelle is called the powerhouse of the cell?

CHAPTER 3

ABOVE, BELOW, AND BEYOND: THE EARTH AND SPACE SCIENCES

It's a clear and dark night. Your dad just picked you up from band practice. You look out the car window. You see a fuzzy patch of light flung across the night sky. That's our galaxy, the Milky Way.

The Milky Way isn't just a candy bar. It is an enormous, spinning collection of stars, planets, dust, and gas. It's all held in place by gravity. Our sun is just one of at least 100 billion stars that make up the Milky Way. The sun seems bigger and brighter than all the rest of the stars. That's because it's the closest—a little less than 93 million miles (150 million kilometers) away!

The sun, Earth, and all of the other planets in our solar system spin on their axes. The Earth and the other planets orbit around the sun. If that makes you dizzy, think of it this way. It's as if you were spinning a basketball—that's the Earth—on your finger as you were walking in a circle around a bright light—the sun.

Each rotation of the basketball represents one day. As the basketball rotates on its axis, different parts face the light at different times. So when one part of the Earth faces the sun, it's daytime in that part of the world. As it turns away from the sun, it becomes evening and then night. It takes 24 hours for the Earth to complete its rotation.

Earth's HISTORY

Do your parents ever show you pictures of you as a baby? You probably wonder how you looked so different back then. The planet Earth looked pretty different in its infancy too.

About 4.6 billion years ago, Earth was just a soupy ball of melted rock and metals—made of elements from exploding stars. The heavier matter, such as nickel and iron, sank into the core region. The lighter stuff floated up to the surface.

It helps to think of the Earth as an egg. The Earth's outer surface, the crust, is made of solid rock. It's like a thin eggshell covering what's inside. Beneath the crust is the mantle. The mantle is made of hot melted rock. Like the egg white, it can be squished around.

Beneath the mantle is the outer core, about 3,000 miles (4,800 km) beneath Earth's surface. You can think of it as the outer part of the yolk, except this stuff is made of hot, melted metal, mostly iron and nickel. The inner core, made mostly of iron, is like a super-hot, spinning inner yolk.

QUICK TIP

The Earth's crust is about 6 miles (10 km) thick below the ocean floor and 37 miles (60 km) thick below the continents.

Bonus Point

The inner core of the Earth is somewhere between 9,000 and 13,000 degrees Fahrenheit (5,000 to 7,200 degrees Celsius). Yet the iron inside cannot melt. Do you know why?

EARTH'S SYSTEMS

If you are on a sports team, you know that every member has a different position to play. If you're the forward for your basketball team, you've probably developed some pretty good dribbling skills. But you can't win a game without your teammates. Everyone has to work together.

The same goes for Earth. Earth actually consists of four systems that all work together: the geosphere, the atmosphere, the hydrosphere, and the biosphere.

The Geosphere

The geosphere includes the Earth's core, mantle, and crust. They contain all the rocks, minerals, and landforms on Earth. You might think that rocks just sit around and do nothing, but the geosphere is actually very active. The Earth's crust is made up of separate plates, or giant slabs of solid rock. They float over the molten rock underneath and shift over time. This is called the tectonic plate theory.

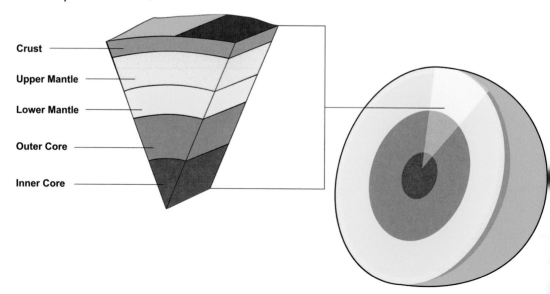

Crust
Upper Mantle
Lower Mantle
Outer Core
Inner Core

North America

Eurasia

South America

Africa

Antarctica

Australia

QUICK TIP

Tectonic comes from the Greek word meaning "to build."

At one time all of Earth's landforms were joined together in one supercontinent called Pangaea. Around 200 million years ago, that supercontinent began to split into pieces. They eventually drifted apart and formed the continents we have today. Take a look at the globe. It's easy to see how the continents used to fit together, like pieces of a puzzle.

TECTONIC PLATES

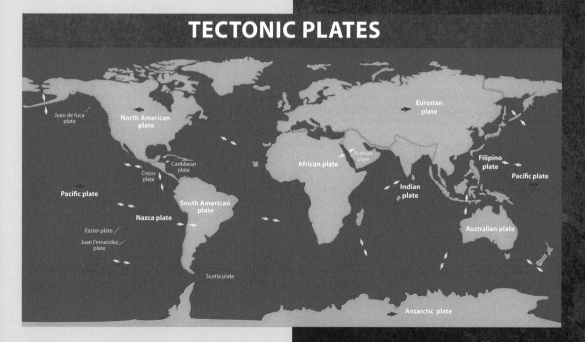

Juan de fuca plate

North American plate

Eurasian plate

Caribbean plate

Arabian plate

African plate

Filipino plate

Pacific plate

Cocos plate

Indian plate

Pacific plate

South American plate

Nazca plate

Australian plate

Easter plate

Juan Fernandez plate

Scotia plate

Antarctic plate

The ATMOSPHERE

Take a deep breath. You've just inhaled some atmosphere! The atmosphere is the blanket of gas molecules surrounding the Earth. It consists mostly of nitrogen and oxygen. Other very important trace gases, including ozone, methane, and carbon dioxide are also a part of the atmosphere. These are sometimes called greenhouse gases. They help trap heat from the sun. The atmosphere also helps block harmful radiation from the sun.

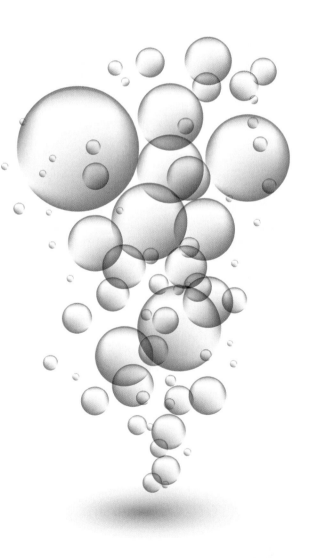

Light as air? You may be surprised to learn that, at sea level, the atmosphere actually presses down with so much force it's like carrying a small car on your body! Don't worry about getting squashed. You have gases inside your body that push back outward at the same pressure.

If you've ever been to the top of a tall mountain, you may notice that your ears pop. That's because the atmosphere gets thinner as you go higher. There are fewer air molecules pressing down on you, and your ears pop to balance the pressure inside and out. It's also more difficult to breathe since there's less oxygen up there.

The HYDROSPHERE

You can't live without water. The water you drink was first a part of the hydrosphere. The hydrosphere includes all of the ice, water vapor, and liquid water on Earth and in the sky. Water is constantly on the move, from the atmosphere to the geosphere and back again. This is known as the water cycle.

The heat from the sun causes water from oceans, lakes, rivers, and plants to evaporate. It's turned into water vapor, which rises up into the atmosphere. The cold air turns the gas back into droplets of liquid, which form clouds. When the clouds get so filled with water they can't hold any more, it rains, snows, sleets, or hails. Then the water cycle starts over again.

The Water Cycle

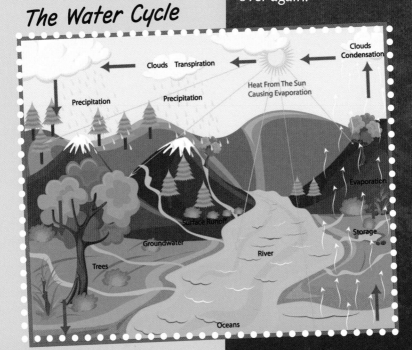

Water is essential for all living things, but it also has a huge impact on the land. Rushing rivers wear away at their banks, carving out valleys and caves. It took the Colorado River a mere 5 million years to carve out the Grand Canyon. Pounding ocean waves reduce pebbles to sand and erode seaside cliffs. Huge slabs of ice called glaciers carved much of the landscape in the northern part of North America.

QUICK TIP

Less than 3 percent of the hydrosphere is fresh water. Most of this is stored in glaciers and ice caps at the North and South Poles. Most of the Earth's water is found in the oceans, which are salt water and cover nearly 70 percent of the Earth's surface.

THE BIOSPHERE

Live it up! The biosphere is all about life, from the tiniest microbe to the ginormous blue whale. You'll find living things in the darkest depths of the ocean and high up in the clouds. Some organisms thrive in water hot enough to burn people. Others live inside freezing, icy glaciers. We're all adapted to our own special niches here on Earth.

Sometimes conditions on Earth change. When that happens, some species just can't adapt. They go extinct. In fact, more than 90 percent of all things that ever lived on Earth are now extinct. Sometimes this is caused by drastic climate change. That's what happened to the dinosaurs. Other species, like the passenger pigeon, went extinct because people hunted them and destroyed their habitats. Scientists have identified around 1.9 million different species of living things. However, they estimate that there are many millions more species that are yet to be discovered.

QUICK TIP

Need a quick way to remember the earth's systems—the geosphere, hydrosphere, atmosphere, and biosphere? How about this: Girls Have Amazing Brains.

Earth AND Human Activity

Think of the Earth's systems—the geosphere, the atmosphere, the hydrosphere, and the biosphere—as Team Earth. The atmosphere interacts with the oceans to create weather and climate patterns. Icy-cold or warm ocean currents move between the poles and the equator, cooling or warming the air above. Mountains can block clouds and winds. Plants remove some of the carbon dioxide from the atmosphere. On Team Earth every member works together to keep things in balance.

There's plenty of evidence showing that humans are having a big impact on how Team Earth works. And not in a good way. When CO_2 and other greenhouse gases are in balance, they keep our planet's temperature at a "Goldilocks" level. Not too hot, not too cold.

By burning fossil fuels to power our cars, factories, and power plants, we release CO_2. This puts a lot more heat-trapping gases into the atmosphere. It's changing the Earth's climate in a dramatic way.

Over the last century, Earth's average temperature has risen about 1.53°F (0.85°C). That may not seem like much, but it has a huge effect. Air and ocean temperatures are warming. Glaciers are melting. Sea levels are rising. Global warming doesn't just mean that the Earth is becoming warmer. It also means that rainfall and flooding are becoming heavier. Droughts and heat waves are growing worse. Hurricanes and other storms are becoming stronger.

On Earth humans aren't always the best team players. We pollute the air, the oceans, and the land. We destroy other animals' habitats. We use more than our share of Earth's resources. Fortunately, many scientists are figuring out how we can work better with Team Earth.

Engineers are developing better ways to use energy that doesn't pollute the atmosphere. Many communities in the U.S. and elsewhere have recycling programs to reduce the amount of waste we put into the landfills. Animal rights groups are working hard to protect endangered species by restoring critical habitats.

Experiment

Tell time without a watch—build a sundial!

You'll need:
- a straight stick about 2 feet (60 centimeters) long
- 12 pebbles or small seashells
- a watch

Steps:

Find a sunny spot in your yard. Push the stick straight into the soil. No yard? No problem. Just fill a small bucket with sand, and place your stick in the bucket.

Start in the morning when the sun is up. At 7:00 a.m. use a pebble to mark the place where the shadow of your stick falls. Do the same on the hour, every hour, until there is no more daylight left. At the end of the day you will have created a sundial! If you ran out of daylight, place your remaining pebbles or seashells about where you think they should go. As long as the sun is shining, you won't need your watch. If you keep your sundial up for several months, you'll notice that the length of the shadows change throughout the seasons. Do you know why?

Science Savvy at Work

Marjorie Chan, Professor of Geology, University of Utah

Dr. Marjorie Chan is a sedimentary geologist who looks at layered strata, or layers of rocks. "Utah has spectacular exposures that people from all over the world come to see," Dr. Chan said. "It is a beautiful landscape with many stories of past environments that are preserved like pages in a book."

One of the things that Dr. Chan most enjoys about being a geologist is the chance to work outdoors and learn about the landscape wherever she travels. "There is a sense of adventure when I go out to study rocks," she says.

Dr. Chan's advice: "If you like learning new things all the time it's hard to find anything as thrilling, challenging, and rewarding as geology. Your life will be full and you will meet a lot of fascinating people and share many amazing experiences."

TEST YOUR SCIENCE SAVVY

1. Pretend you are a drop of water. Keep a travel journal as you make your way through the water cycle. Where did you go? How long did you stay at each stage? Did you meet any friends or enemies?

2. On April 10, 1815, Mount Tambora, a volcano on an island in the Pacific Ocean erupted. It was the worst volcanic eruption in 10,000 years, killing many people immediately. But it also spewed out tons of gas, ash, and dust into the atmosphere. The following year became known as "The Year Without Summer." Unusually cold weather in North America and Europe killed crops, leading to widespread famine. Can you explain what caused the Earth's temperatures to plunge so dramatically?

CHAPTER 4

ENGINEERING: DESIGNING A NEW WAY TO COMMUNICATE WITH YOUR FRIENDS

Physics, chemistry, biology, geology—they're all ways of investigating the fascinating world around us. Engineering takes all of that cool info and puts it to work. If you like science and you're problem solver who likes to make or design things, engineering might be in your future. How would you engineer a new way to communicate with your BFF? Follow these four steps.

1. Identify a Problem in Search of a Solution

Imagine you live next door to your best friend. Your bedrooms are both on the second floor, facing each other. You want to set up a system to communicate with each other that doesn't involve cell phones or shouting. (After all, some things are private.) Think about your options ...

2. Brainstorm

You and a friend get together for a brainstorming session. After all, two heads are better than one. You could ...

- fly paper airplanes carrying messages back and forth.
- throw a tennis ball with an attached message between windows.
- throw a line across the two windows and set up a pulley system to transfer messages.
- learn Morse code, an alphabetic code using a combination of long and short signals. Use drumsticks to tap out the signals on your windowsills. Or make up your own code, one that only you and your friend can understand.

3. Develop and Test Possible Designs

- The paper airplane was a great idea until the wind delivered your secret messages into the hands of your little brother. Fail!
- You pitch for your softball team, so you've got a pretty good arm. But your friend? She's got a lot of talents, but catching isn't one of them. Fail!
- You manage to set up a pulley system between your rooms. It works great! But your parents aren't too crazy about having a clothesline strung between the two houses. Sadly, another fail.
- Learning Morse code is easy. It's fun too once you get the hang of it! The two of you can communicate pretty well, but your sister complains about the noise. Is there a way you can send signals more quietly?

4. Tweak and tinker with your design to make it better.

- You experiment with flashlights and find that they work great! Problem solved. That's a

● — — ● ● — ●

("WIN" in Morse code!) You've just engineered your own way to communicate with your friend.

Science Savvy at Work

Tanya Martinez, Energy Engineer at 7thGen Energy, Phoenix, Arizona

Dr. Tanya Martinez works on developing and building renewable energy projects. Most of the energy we use today comes from burning fossil fuels like coal and gas, which hurt the environment.

Renewable energy, on the other hand, comes from resources like the sun that lasts forever (unlike coal or gas). It's better for the environment.

Dr. Martinez's advice? If you're considering engineering, do it! "Engineering is in every aspect of our lives," she says. "All you need to do is figure out what you care about, appreciate, or are passionate about. We like to make a difference and engineering provides an opportunity to do that."

WHAT DO ENGINEERS DO?

There are so many careers in engineering design. Here are just a few.

- **Aerospace engineers** design and develop aircraft, from gliders to spaceships.
- **Biomedical engineers** focus on ways to help treat medical problems. One example is creating better artificial limbs.
- **Chemical engineers** use their knowledge of chemistry to make better fuels, clean up pollution, or even to make better-tasting food!

- **Civil engineers** design and supervise the creation of structures, including bridges, roads, tunnels, or buildings.
- **Computer and software engineers** use and develop new computer hardware and software. They're the ones behind all of your electronic gadgets.
- **Electrical engineers** design, develop, and maintain a wide range of electrical systems and equipment. They work with everything from tiny electronic circuits to huge communications satellites.

- **Environmental engineers** work to make sure that polluting chemicals are not released into our air or water supply, and that solid waste is safely disposed.
- **Industrial engineers** are sometimes called "efficiency experts." They figure out how to make complex systems, and especially large companies, work better.
- **Materials engineers** figure out how to use technology to make cool new stuff, such as more flexible snowboards or lightweight warm clothing.

- **Mechanical engineers** design and make all kinds of nifty devices like tools, engines, and machines.
- **Nuclear engineers** harness the power of nuclear energy and radiation. They may work at nuclear power stations or even develop better medical imaging devices.

Soar with Science

Science is all around you. It's in the food you eat, the sports you play, and inside your body. Maybe you dream of discovering new life under the sea or inventing a new smartphone. Or maybe you just want to finally get an A in your science class. Remember science doesn't have to be just a subject you study in school. It can be a way of life you use to explore and create.

TEST YOUR SCIENCE SAVVY

Match the technology with the type of engineer to develop it. In many cases, several different kinds of engineers contributed to the technology. But can you figure out the primary engineering influence?

1. aerospace engineer
2. biomedical engineer
3. chemical engineer
4. civil engineer
5. computer and software engineer
6. electrical engineer
7. environmental engineer
8. industrial engineer
9. materials engineer
10. mechanical engineer
11. nuclear engineer

A. design new toys for kids

B. create the space shuttle

C. make new swimsuits that are faster and sleeker

D. develop user-friendly software for bloggers

E. design schools that are more comfortable for students and teachers

F. invent better ways of recycling plastic

G. build a bionic leg that can be controlled with thoughts

H. make biofuels from algae

I. create special effects for the movies

J. inspect and evaluate the safety of nuclear power plants

K. build low-cost, sturdy structures for victims of hurricanes and flooding

ANSWER KEY

Chapter 1

Experiment: Blow it up!

You just made a chemical reaction between two reactants—vinegar (a liquid) and baking soda (a solid). Vinegar is actually acetic acid mixed with water. It contains two atoms of carbon, four atoms of hydrogen, and two atoms of oxygen: $C_2H_4O_2$. Baking soda is made of one atom each of sodium, hydrogen, carbon, and three atoms of oxygen: $NaHCO_3$. These two substances react and recombine to make sodium acetate, water, and carbon dioxide:

$$NaHCO_3 + C_2H_4O_2 \longrightarrow NaC_2H_3O_2 + H_2O + CO_2$$

It's the carbon dioxide gas that made your balloon inflate!

If you added more baking soda, you probably created more gas and saw more foam, right? That's because you're adding more reactants. Less means less gas and foam.

Experiment: Energy Transfer in Action!

When you held the two balls up in the air, they both had potential energy. When you dropped them, they gained kinetic energy. When the larger ball hit the ground, it transferred its kinetic energy to the smaller ball, sending it flying into the air. Energy is never lost, only transferred into other kinds of energy.

Experiment: Make Waves!

As your clothing tumbled in the dryer, some items gained a positive charge, while others gained a negative charge. Electromagnetic forces caused them to cling together. When you pulled them apart, they gave off small sparks—and those sparks produced radio waves!

Test Your Science Savvy Answers

1. The First Law of Motion: An object in motion will stay in motion and an object at rest will stay at rest unless acted upon by an unbalanced force. When you're traveling in a car, you're traveling at the same speed as the car. If the driver has to slam on the brakes, you would continue traveling forward if it weren't for the restraining force of your seat belt.

2. Electromagnetic wave—the only part of the electromagnetic spectrum that we can see. When sunlight shines on raindrops in just the right way, the water bends the light waves as it moves through the drops. It separates out the red, orange, yellow, green, blue, indigo, and violet—all different wavelengths—to create a rainbow. You can do the same thing by shining a light on a prism. If you've ever noticed how a straw in a glass of water seems bent where the water meets the air, you've seen another example of bendy light waves.

3. The force of friction acts upon the softball player.

Chapter 2

Bonus Point

Some examples of other types of cells include bone, liver, nerve, and egg. There are many more!

Test Your Science Savvy Answers

1. A mule, the offspring of a horse and donkey, cannot reproduce. Fire, on the other hand, uses energy, grows, and can reproduce.

2. The correct answer is C. The Venus flytrap is both a producer and a consumer. All plants need sunlight, water, and carbon dioxide. In order to grow, they also need nutrients such as nitrogen, phosphorus, and iron. Most plants get these materials from the soil. But carnivorous plants such as the Venus flytrap live in places where there's not many nutrients in the soil. They get those nutrients from insects instead!

3. Sunlight, water, and carbon dioxide.

4. Mitochondria

Chapter 3

Bonus Point

The pressure bearing down on the inner core from the entire planet is so great that the iron molecules cannot move around. They are squeezed together in a solid.

Experiment

You probably noticed that the shadows grow longer in the winter and shorter in the summer. Due to the tilt in the Earth's axis, the sun's rays are more angled during the winter months, and more direct during the summer months.

Test Your Science Savvy Answers

1. Your travels should have taken you to the atmosphere, the oceans, rivers, or streams, underground, and through living things. Did you remember to change states, from solid to liquid to vapor?

2. The volcano's gas, ash, and dust rose high into the atmosphere, forming a kind of cloud the size of Australia. The cloud, which drifted across the globe, reflected much of the sun's rays back into space, resulting in a nasty, cold summer.

Chapter 4

1. B	5. D	9. C
2. G	6. I	10. A
3. H	7. F	11. J
4. K	8. E	

GLOSSARY

acceleration (ak-sel-uh-RAY-shuhn)—the increase in speed of a moving body

atom (AT-uhm)—an element in its smallest form

ecosystem (EE-koh-sis-tuhm)—a system of living and nonliving things in an environment

energy (E-nuhr-jee)—the ability to do work, such as moving things or giving heat or light

erode (i-ROHD)—to gradually wear away

force (FORS)—any action that changes the movement of an object

friction (FRIK-shuhn)—a force created when two objects rub together; friction slows down objects.

global warming (GLOHB-uhl WARM-eeng)—rise in the average worldwide temperature

gravity (GRAV-uh-tee)—a force that pulls objects with mass together; gravity pulls objects down toward the center of Earth

habitat (HAB-uh-tat)—the natural place and conditions in which a plant or animal lives

mass (MASS)—the amount of material in an object

matter (MAT-ur)—anything that has weight and takes up space

molecule (MOL-uh-kyool)—the atoms making up the smallest unit of a substance; H_2O is a molecule of water.

mutation (myoo-TAY-shun)—a change in genetic material

natural selection (NACH-ur-uhl sell-ECK-shun)—the process in which the organisms best adapted to their environment survive

nucleus (NYOO-klee-uhss)—the center of an atom or cell

photosynthesis (foh-toh-SIN-thuh-siss)—the process by which green plants make their food

tectonic plate (tek-TON-ik PLAYT)—gigantic slab of Earth's crust that moves around on magma

READ MORE

Lew, Kristi, *Cool Biology Activities for Girls*. Mankato, Minn.: Capstone Press, 2012.

Schwartz, Heather E., *Cool Engineering Activities for Girls*. Mankato, Minn.: Capstone Press, 2012.

Slade, Suzanne, *Cool Physics Activities for Girls*. Mankato, Minn.: Capstone Press, 2012.

Wheeler-Toppen, Jodi, *Cool Chemistry Activities for Girls*. Mankato, Minn.: Capstone Press, 2012.

INTERNET SITES

FactHound offers a safe, fun way to find Internet sites related to this book. All of the sites on FactHound have been researched by our staff.

Here's all you do:

Visit *www.facthound.com*

Type in this code: 9781491407721

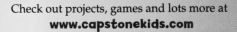

Super-cool stuff! Check out projects, games and lots more at **www.capstonekids.com**

INDEX